Let's Cook!

by Arlène Elizabeth Casimir • illustrated by Yulia Gorkina

Lucy Calkins and Michael Rae-Grant, Series Editors

Let's Cook!
Author: Arlène Elizabeth Casimir
Series Editors: Lucy Calkins and Michael Rae-Grant

Heinemann
145 Maplewood Avenue, Suite 300
Portsmouth, NH 03801
www.heinemann.com

Cataloging-in-Publication data is on file with the Library of Congress.

ISBN-13: 978-0-325-13832-9

Design and Production: Dinardo Design LLC, Carole Berg, and Rebecca Anderson

Editors: Anna Cockerille and Jennifer McKenna

Illustrations: Yulia Gorkina

Photographs: p. 32 (Haitian food) © Darsen/Shutterstock; inside back cover (boy in checked shirt) © ViDI Studio/Shutterstock; inside back cover (socks) © Marek Mnich/Shutterstock.

Manufacturing: Gerard Clancy

Printed in Dongguan, China
4 5 6 7 8 9 10 TP 28 27 26 25 24 23
April 2023 Printing / PO# 4500868396

Contents

Meet...

Lalin

Liv

Bel

Mom

Dad

Will You Help?

"Will you help me cook?"
asks Mom.

Dad has to dust,

so he can not help.

Can Bel and Liv help?

Bel and Liv CAN, but...

"I will help!" says Lalin.

"OK," says Mom.

"Let's cook the griot.

Go grab the pot!"

Rub,
rub,
rub!

"Add it in," says Mom.

Lalin and Mom let it sit.

In a bit, Mom says,

"Let's get it in the pot."

"Mmm! Mmm!" says Dad.
"I can smell the griot! Yum!"

2

Hiss! Crack! Pop!

"Next, we will cook the rice," says Mom.

"Will you get up and help me?"
asks Mom.

"Lalin, you can go and get the rice," says Mom.

Lalin lifts up the big bag of rice.

She hands the bag to Mom.

Mom cuts off a bit of fat
to toss in the pan.
Sssssss! It melts so fast.

"Liv, you can add the mix,"
says Mom.

"Bel, you can add the rice,"
says Mom.

Hiss! Crack!

The rice pops and snaps.

Mom hugs the kids and says,
"I am so, so glad you kids
can help me cook!"

3

Griot, Rice, and Yams

Lalin can smell

the griot, the rice, and the yams.

Yum! Yum! Yum!

Mom and Dad sit...

and the kids sit too.

"Yum! Pass me the griot!"
says Dad.

"Pass it to me too!" says Lalin.

"Just rice and yams for me,"
says Liv.

"Me too," says Bel.

"Just rice and yams. No griot."

"OK," says Dad.

"YOU can get rice and yams,

and WE can get lots and lots
and LOTS of griot!"

HAITIAN FOOD

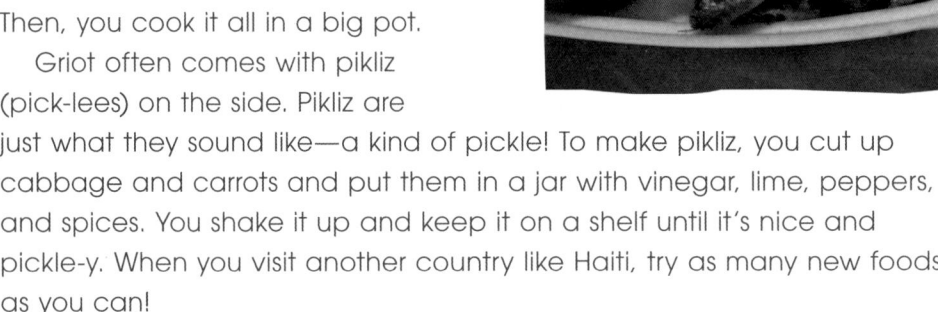
pikliz

griot

Time for dinner! Look at that plate full of Haitian food. *Bon apeti!*

Every country and culture has special foods. In this book, Lalin and her mom cook Haitian griot (gree-owe). To make griot, you cover pork or jackfruit in lemon juice, lime juice, peppers, onions, garlic, and epis (ay-peace), a mix of spices. Then, you cook it all in a big pot.

Griot often comes with pikliz (pick-lees) on the side. Pikliz are just what they sound like—a kind of pickle! To make pikliz, you cut up cabbage and carrots and put them in a jar with vinegar, lime, peppers, and spices. You shake it up and keep it on a shelf until it's nice and pickle-y. When you visit another country like Haiti, try as many new foods as you can!

Talk about...

Ask your reader some questions like...

- What happened in this book?
- Why didn't Lalin's sisters help at first?
- How do you think Mom felt when Lalin helped?

- Lalin likes to help other people. Think about a time when *you* helped someone. How did you help? How did it feel when you helped?